Maximizing The Pareto Principle

The Secret Strategy to Optimizing Every Area of Your Life

Sensei Paul David

Copyright Page

Maximizing The Pareto Principle: The Secret Strategy to Optimizing Every Area of Your Life, by Sensei Paul David

Copyright © 2022

All rights reserved.

978-1-77848-074-4 SSD_Maximizing The ParetoPrinciple_Ingram_Paperback

978-1-77848-073-7 SSD_Maximizing The ParetoPrinciple_Amazon_PaperbackBook

978-1-77848-072-0 SSD_Maximizing The ParetoPrinciple_Amazon_eBook

This book is not authorized for free distribution copying.

www.senseipublishing.com

@senseipublishing
#senseipublishing

Get/Share Our FREE All-Ages Mental Health Book Now!

FREE Self-Development Book for Every Family

senseiselfdevelopment.senseipublishing.com

Click Below or Search Amazon for Another Book In This Series

Join Our Publishing Journey!

If you would like to receive FUTURE FREE BOOKS and get to know us better, please click www.senseipublishing.com and join our newsletter by entering your email address in the pop-up box.

Follow Our Blog: senseipauldavid.ca

Follow/Like/Subscribe: Facebook, Instagram, YouTube: @senseipublishing

Scan the QR Code with your phone or tablet
to follow us on social media: Like / Subscribe / Follow

Thank You from The Author: Sensei Paul David

Before we dive in, I would like to thank you for picking up this book from among the many other similar books out there. Thank you for choosing to invest in my book. That means everything to me.

Now that you are here, I ask you to stick with me as we take your self-discovery journey together. I promise to make our time together valuable and worthwhile.

In the pages ahead, you will find some areas of information and practices more helpful than others - and that is great! I encourage you to apply what works best for you. You will benefit from the knowledge that you gain and the ensuing exciting transformation of character.

Enjoy!

Table of Contents

Introduction 1

Chapter One: The Pareto Principle 3

   Introduction To The Pareto Principle 3

   Life Is Unfair 6

   Working Smart 8

Chapter Two: Leveraging The Pareto Principle In Your Career 12

   Prioritizing Your Area Of Concentration 12

Chapter Three: Taking Advantage Of The Pareto Principle In Stress Management 21

   Recognizing Your Most Significant Stressors 22

   Financial Pressure 23

   Children As Stressors 25

   Your Job As A Stressor 29

Chapter Four: Leveraging The Pareto Principle In Goal Setting 32

   Setting Targets That Matter 32

   Pick Your Battles Wisely 35

   Applying The Pareto Principle To Goal Setting 37

Chapter Five: Leveraging The Pareto Principle In Your Interpersonal Relationships 40

   The Loss of Empathy In The Modern World 41

   Existing In A Community 43

The Pareto Principle In Your Relationships 45

Chapter Six: Leveraging The Pareto Principle In Your Marriage 48

What Is Wrong With Our Marriages? 49

Learning From The Right Models 51

The Pareto Effect On Your Marriage 53

Chapter Seven: Leveraging The Pareto Principle In Leadership 57

Leadership Is Key 57

Leading With The Pareto Principle 59

Chapter Eight: Leveraging The Pareto Principle To Find Meaning And Happiness 66

Happiness or Success 67

The Pareto Principle Formula For Happiness 69

Conclusion 74

References 76

Foreword

The Pareto Principle has been around for a while. However, it is still a novel idea that is both fascinating and effective. Yet, it is predominantly applied to businesses. In *Maximizing The Pareto Principle*, Paul shows us that we do not have to restrict its application to business only. This book teaches how we can use this model in every area of our lives.

In this short, classic self-development and mental health book, Paul simplified this principle and showed us its potential practical application in our careers and interpersonal relationships. This guide is like a fire extinguisher that can help readers to put out the flames of lack of productivity by discovering the reasons for their inefficiencies. This is a must-read for anyone seeking to do less while achieving more.

Introduction

"Productivity is never an accident. It is always the result of a commitment to excellence, intelligent planning, and focused effort."

Paul J. Meyer

When people do not understand the secret to the success of a person, they attribute it to luck or wrongly assume that the person is doing something illicit or illegal. Life can be frustrating when you are not working smart. Life will not always give you what you want but you can make life easier for yourself when you discover more effective ways to achieve your targets.

People will always rightly encourage you to work your socks off to achieve success. Yet, the truth is that life can seem unfair sometimes. The fact that you put several hours into something does not mean it will necessarily end well. In the same way, the fact that you are committed to a relationship does not mean your partner will always be faithful to you.

The secret to achieving more in life is to find smarter ways to get the job done. This book is based on the Pareto Principle, which states that 80% of the results in life are products of 20% of input. This guide will teach you how you can leverage this principle to achieve more while doing less in every aspect of your life.

Chapter One: The Pareto Principle

According to economist Vilfredo Pareto, 80% of the occurrences in life are due to 20% of the causes. This is known as the Pareto principle. You can leverage this principle to enhance your productivity in your career and interpersonal relationships. This chapter will explore this principle and its practical application.

Introduction To The Pareto Principle

Economist, Vilfredo Pareto, discovered that 80% of the land in Italy was owned by 20% of the population. In his further research, he observed that this pattern was replicated across Europe. The Pareto principle was derived from this observation of the uneven distribution of wealth. This is still true today and is even worse. According to *PolitiFact*, the wealth of the 400 wealthiest Americans is more than half of the wealth of all Americans combined! Things might not change any time soon because most of these people inherited their wealth and will still pass it on to their children and families, and so it will continue.

Inequality All-Around

In *Dear God*, rapper Dax aired his frustration when he stated that he could not understand why some people have over a hundred million dollars in their savings account, while there are people on the street who cannot even afford their daily meals. Indeed, the Pareto Principle is based on the alarming inequality in the world today. Yet, you can use it to your advantage when you understand its practical application. For example, it has been discovered that 20% of the employees of a company are usually responsible for 80% of its profits.

Also, a combination of nations like India, China, Japan, Russia, Nigeria, and the US makes up more than half of the population of the world. There is usually a higher concentration somewhere in every endeavour in life. You might not like this fact but it is the reality of the world we live in. In *12 Rules For Life*, author Jordan Petersen analyzed the unfair nature of life where certain people occupy the top of the ladder of various endeavours in life due to a combination of inheritance and coincidences while others have to struggle and fight to achieve anything monumental.

His counsel is that you should accept this reality and find a way to navigate your way to the top because it can frustrate you and shorten your life if you don't. This also applies to the issue of racism. Racism is alive and kicking in the US and most parts of Europe. Indeed, efforts should be made to curb this menace but the victims have to accept this reality and find ways to be happy and live a meaningful life amid the anomaly until things get better.

Life Is Unfair

Life can be so unfair that it makes many people tempted to leave things to chance. The fact that it took you four years to achieve something does not mean that someone else will not achieve it within four months. This is the irony of life. In the modern world, we have several machines that help us to achieve more without putting in the same effort as our ancestors. Imagine the dilemma of early human beings to make fire. However, we have become "fire lords" today. We can start a fire with just a snap of our fingers now, thanks to technological advancement.

This is reminiscent of every aspect of our lives today. We do not have to spend weeks or months travelling on foot or horses anymore. You can get to any continent today, regardless of where you are around the world, within a matter of hours. We are not working as hard as our ancestors today because we are working smarter than they did or could. Of course, you might argue the downsides of living in the modern world but the fact is that there has never been any time in the history of humanity where we have been this smart and sleek. The next few years also offer even more breakthroughs in science and technology. Indeed, we are fortunate in several respects to be part of the modern world.

The Chelsea-Bayern Case Study

The UEFA Champions League Final between Chelsea and Bayern Munich is a perfect depiction of how life can be unfair sometimes. During the match, Bayern had 43 shots on goal, with 7 on target, while Chelsea had 9 shots on goal, with 3 on target. Bayern had 20 corner kicks, while Chelsea only had one. Guess what? Chelsea scored from their only corner kick, and the match ended as a one-all draw at the end of 90 minutes.

Bayern had scored earlier, while Chelsea scored at the very end when all hopes were almost gone. In extra time, Bayern had a penalty but missed, and Chelsea eventually won the match after a penalty shootout. Many people praise the resilience of that Chelsea side but that game is a classic example of how things can go wrong when there are several reasons they should end well.

Working Smart

There is no point in decrying the unfair nature of life. Rather, you should leverage it to make the best you can out of your life. Many of us are wired to believe that we can only get the best out of life by working extremely hard but this is not always the case. Working smart is better than working hard. During my college days, a colleague called me to ask how I seemed to be getting good grades without working as hard as she did. I understood her confusion. She worked hard by spending a significant part of her day in the library whenever we did not have lectures. However, her grades were not matching her efforts. Initially, she assumed that it was because I was more intelligent.

Nonetheless, she summoned the courage to ask me to enlighten her on how she could get good grades like me. During our conversation, she discovered that what gave me an advantage was my method. She discovered that I was not just studying but I was more conscious of the psychology of the lecturer. I would draw out every possible question from the materials we were given and answer the questions instead of trying to cram the information. Therefore, I spent more time answering the questions rather than reading the materials and my grades were usually superb. Many of my colleagues adopted my method and it improved their grades.

By leveraging the Pareto Principle, you can make smart decisions in every aspect of your life, including leadership, goal setting, stress management, interpersonal relationships, marriage, and career choices. In the subsequent chapters, we will analyze how you can take advantage of this principle to live the happy and meaningful life that you desire and deserve. Once you spot those areas of concentration in your life, you will be more productive and happier. It will help you to note the least productive aspects of your life and limit your investment in those. Time is a resource you cannot control and cannot afford to waste. Therefore, you must find ways to maximize your time and effort on the most productive and meaningful aspects of your life.

Chapter Two: Leveraging The Pareto Principle In Your Career

"Find out what you like doing best, and get someone to pay you for doing it."
                    Katharine Whitehorn

Prioritizing Your Area Of Concentration

Remember, that the crux of the Pareto Principle is to discover your area of concentration. In other words, find out the most productive aspects of your life and invest most parts of your effort in them. You can apply this principle to your career in the following ways:

Discover Your Passion

Our jobs are crucial aspects of our lives. According to Pew Research Center, over 50% of Americans identify themselves based on their job description. Sadly, more than one-half of all American employees are disengaged at work. This is a cause for concern. You should not find yourself in a job you do not want to do. The truth is that every job is stressful in one way or the other. However, you can increase your chances of job satisfaction when you are passionate about your job.

The words of Katharine Whitehorn at the beginning of this chapter, sum up the best approach to making career choices. When you find something you love to do, it will maximize your talent and abilities. It will allow you to be comfortable and give your best every day. Emmanuel Kant vehemently castigated the tendency to treat human beings as machines in the workplace. Sadly, this is what many people have become. They only work to earn money without consideration for their mental and physical health. Discovering your passion and making a career out of it solves most of these problems.

Prioritize Your Passion

As a college student, I joined a group of colleagues who were passionate about helping one another improve academically. It was a new lease on life for me. It helped me to showcase my academic prowess and help others improve, which has always been my passion. This is the same reason I write self-help books. However, at some point, the leader of the group started deviating from the main objective. He wanted us to explore extracurricular activities.

I guess he was bored with the routine of pursuing academic excellence. I knew at that point that I could not continue with the group. My priority at that point in my life was academic excellence and I would not allow anything to distract me. I announced my uncomfortable exit from the group and formed a new one that would only focus on academic excellence. Some of the people from the group I left, also joined. In the long run, the leader of the group came to seek my help with his academics. This is the power of focus. Once you discover your passion, it has to become your priority. Get rid of distractions and focus.

Invest in Your Passion

Whatever is worth doing at all is worth doing well. If you are not willing to invest your time, energy, and money in a career, it is not worth doing. Your job is your means of sustenance and it provides the resources that will help you to contribute positively to the lives of others. Therefore, you should not take it for granted. Let it be clear to everyone around you that you value your work and will do all you can to succeed.

Read books, attend seminars, and leverage the mentorship of experienced people in your field. You need to do this in the early part of your life. Hindus believe that there are four phases of life, known as the *ashramas*. *Brahmacharya*, which is the first phase, is the first twenty-five years of life. It should be dedicated to discovering your passion, learning, and investing heavily in it.

Share Your Passion With Others

It is easy to get intimidated in a world where certain career paths and roles attract more respect than others. Yet, every job is critical to the functioning of our society. How would we cope if everyone were to become doctors and lawyers? Who would cultivate the farms and get us food? People who dedicate their time to taking care of adults or teaching children are hardly recognized because they are not earning a lot of money.

Yet, you should be proud of your job. If it is not something you are proud of sharing with others, there is no point in committing yourself to it. You should be able to stand proud and tall, wherever you are, to talk about your profession as an expert in that field, regardless of the perception of others.

Enjoy Your Work

In a tweet in the early part of 2020, rapper Nicki Minaj stated that she wasted three months of her life because she did not allow herself to enjoy the moment. Even when you are working your dream job, you might still struggle to be happy when you do not make every moment count.

Celebrate every milestone and let the satisfaction of the moment overwhelm you.

Remind yourself every day that you are doing one of the most important jobs in the world. Be proud of yourself, even as you make plans to make progress. Life is too short for negative energy and emotions. Even during dark days, find reasons to be grateful for your career. It is the least you can do for yourself in the ultra-competitive modern world.

Reevaluate Your Decision

It is great to discover your passion and make a career out of it. Nonetheless, it is also critical, to be honest with yourself and explore a new career path when you no longer have the ability to perform excellently in a job you were passionate about. Failure to do this leads to frustration and depression because it can make you lose relevance. In "From Strength To Strength," author Arthur Brooks discusses the importance of knowing when to transition to a career path that allows you to leverage your crystallized intelligence.

He explains that your fluid intelligence is your ability to solve tough problems and come up with novel ideas, while your crystallized intelligence is your ability to use your knowledge and experience to solve problems. Our fluid intelligence gets worse as we grow older while our crystallized intelligence improves with age. Brooks wanted to become the greatest French horn player of all time. It was his passion and he was dedicated to the craft. However, he found out at some point that his skills were declining no matter how hard he tried.

Eventually, he pursued a career as a social scientist which would allow him to serve humanity through his knowledge. It is never too late to choose a new career path that will allow you to maximize your ability. The law of gravity also applies to our careers. It rises high only to decline again. Even if you are Lionel Messi, you cannot play football forever. The glory will wane and criticism will get louder if you do not quit. The end of a curve is the beginning of a new one that will make you productive and happy if you learn to discover the onset of your decline as quickly as possible.

Chapter Three: Taking Advantage Of The Pareto Principle In Stress Management

We had to physically be in contact with people to become stressed out before now. However, the advent of social media has changed that. We have more stressors in the modern world than ever before. Meanwhile, the lack of stress management can lead to physical and mental exhaustion. It can also make us susceptible to illnesses by weakening our immune system. This chapter will discuss how you can leverage the Pareto Principle in stress management.

Recognizing Your Most Significant Stressors

Stress is inevitable, as long as you have goals you intend to achieve. No pain, no gain. You cannot expect to meet your targets and achieve anything significant in life without experiencing some level of stress. Yet, it has to be managed efficiently to ensure that you do not experience the severe negative impact of poor stress management. To leverage the Pareto Principle in this regard, you need to discover your most significant stressors.

Your stressors can arise from the actions of people, or your schedule. Yet, you must identify them to take the most appropriate action. The reality is that 80% of your stress level is a product of 20% of your stressors. It might be less than that. For example, your stressors could include your job, traffic, spouse, children, relocation, loss of job, the death of a loved one, or your finances. If you pay close attention, you will discover that these stressors vary in their contribution to your stress level, at different points in time.

Financial Pressure

You might notice that finances and traffic are your most significant stressors in a particular month. Your finances alone can even account for over 80% of your stress level during the periods you have financial pressures, such as meeting your rent payment or starting a new business. According to a report by the Global Financial Literacy Excellence Center and University Professor of Economics and Accountancy, 60% of Americans are stressed by their finances while 50% are anxious whenever they have to discuss their finances.

The finding of this study goes a long way toward showing the significant impact of financial pressure on the mental health of the average American. The researchers also discovered that 65% of women are stressed by their financial situation in comparison with 54% of men. Key factors highlighted by the researchers regarding financial pressure include high debt, low financial literacy, insufficient income, and money management challenges. They also discovered that young adults, financially dependent children, and low-income married people are usually the most worried about their finances.

The findings of this study should give you a clue regarding why your finances have a significant impact on your stress levels. It should also give you a clue regarding how to solve the problem. Below are some of the suggested solutions:

- Increase your skill level to enhance your earning ability
- Invest in training and materials that can improve your financial literacy

- Seek professional help regarding the management of your finances
- Improve your spending discipline
- Spend more on assets rather than on liabilities or luxuries items
- Spend based on your budget
- Always have a list when going shopping

Children As Stressors

Movies and real-life experiences will let you know that raising children is one of the most stressful endeavours in life. Children are bundles of energy that excite parents and guardians but they can be grumpy and difficult sometimes. When they are sick, parents are also anxious because of their love for them. According to a 2012 study, published in the Journal of Caring Sciences, approximately 35% of American children are battling stress-related health problems. Meanwhile, unlike most adults, children lack effective stress management skills.

So, when they are stressed, they can be cranky and create a tense atmosphere at home, which stresses their parents and guardians. Parenting is not for anyone that is irresponsible and insensitive. When parents do not know how to handle the rebellion of their children, they resort to crude means of controlling them such as hitting them. Parenting in the modern world has to be deliberate and empathetic. It goes beyond the ability to provide for the needs of the children. Kids are exposed to immoral and unhealthy content on mainstream media and social media today. Therefore, if you are not deliberate about training them, they will be trained by what they observe around them.

In *You Can Blame The Rappers*, rapper Tom MacDonald said:

How many songs about Xanax and alcohol are we dropping?

How many kids we gonna kill 'for we admit it's a problem?

Probably stop if was one of our sons or one of our daughters

We know our demographic is primarily youth

We glorify breaking the law to children in school

Kids copy what we say and imitate what we do

They'll go to jail for doing the things you told em was cool

At some point in the song, he also said:

Half of these artists can't even talk, they just mumble the lyrics

And the teenagers listen while they rebel against their parents

I recommend that you listen to the whole song. It sums up the challenges of raising a kid in the modern world due to the influence and the proliferation of immoral songs popping up left, right, and center. The impact can be devastating if a parent is not careful. No parent can be happy to see their kids become drug addicts or gangsters. Therefore, it is normal that you are tempted to react when you see your children misbehaving. Yet, frustration is not the solution. The following tips can help you in this regard:

- Take time to observe and understand your children because they are unique
- Ensure that you do not speak to your children when you are angry
- Listen more to your kids to earn their trust and understand their

challenges so that you can know how to help them

- Be deliberate about the influences around your kids
- Seek the help of a professional or a more experienced person

Your Job As A Stressor

As mentioned earlier, it is impossible to avoid stress even when you have your dream role in your dream company. So, passion is not enough to save you from job stress. Every occupation has its challenges. You will have to solve problems and meet demands in your role and it can be stressful sometimes. According to the American Institute of Stress, 40% of workers perceive their jobs as extremely stressful. Also, 25% of employees believe that their jobs are their most significant stressors. Therefore, this chapter will not be complete if we do not discuss the impact of your job on your stress level.

In fact, 75% of American employees believe that their roles are more stressful in comparison to a generation ago. Also, 29% of employees admit that they are extremely stressed at work. Therefore, it is evident that the Pareto Principle applies to stress management. Your job alone might account for over 80% of your stress level. Therefore, you must analyze how and why your job places significant stress on you to know how to deal with it. The following tips can be helpful in this regard:

- Review your relationship with your boss and find ways to improve it
- Work on your relationship with your co-workers to build a positive atmosphere in the workplace
- Consider your suitability for your current role

- Seek more effective ways to carry out your duty
- Improve your work-life balance

Chapter Four: Leveraging The Pareto Principle In Goal Setting

Goal setting is an art and you need to learn it. It can be the difference between an average and an excellent year. You cannot underemphasize the role of planning in every achievement and goal setting is a crucial part of that. In this chapter, we will explore how you can take advantage of the Pareto Principle to set goals and actualize your dreams.

Setting Targets That Matter

The heavy influence of social media on the lives of many individuals today has put them in limbo. It is common to find people comparing themselves with others and striving to outdo others. If you are caught in this web, it will make you set targets that will not be important to you in the long run. You should ask yourself at every point the reasons you intend to achieve a goal. If not, you will find yourself acting like a person that lacks direction. Indecision will waste your time and will ensure that you are not consistent in anything.

Stay With Something

It is nothing to write home about when you do not have any particular thing you are engaged in, consistently. Consistency is a sign that you have direction. It is also an essential ingredient in the achievement of any target. The beauty of consistency is that it helps you to discover more effective ways to do something. It helps you to build experience, which helps you to achieve more while doing less. This is the edge experienced people have in jobs, over people that are just learning the ropes.

From your experience, you can tell what works and what will fail. An inexperienced person will employ a trial and error approach, which can be frustrating and time-wasting. On the other hand, an experienced person would have discovered the Pareto Principle in the field. He knows the things you need to do that offer the most significant value. For example, the experience will teach you that it is the satisfaction of your boss that matters the most if you want to enjoy your time while working in a company. Pleasing your co-workers and clients is important too but the boss is the 20% that influences the 80% of your experience in a company.

The American Institute of Stress reported that 35% of American workers see their boss as their main source of stress in the workplace. You might have to quit and find a new job when you struggle to get along well with your employer. Therefore, if you are an employee, pleasing your boss should be one of if not the most important targets you have. His or her happiness will affect your chances of gaining promotion, apart from the great working experience it offers.

Pick Your Battles Wisely

Many people make mistakes when setting goals because their targets are influenced by factors such as envy, revenge, and anger. It is not a good thing to lose your uniqueness amid the rat race many people participate in, in the modern world. When you do not know what you want to do with your life, anyone can ask you to be a volunteer in their plans. You cannot be everything in life, even when you are multi-talented or effective at doing several things. For example, you might have a good voice, excel in sports, and have fantastic academic prowess.

The Rafael Nadal Case Study

If you try to be a top-tier musician, elite sportsperson, and professor at the same time, it is not likely you will excel in any of the three endeavours. For example, Rafael Nadal is one of the greatest tennis players of all time with multiple awards and titles. However, he can also do wonders with his feet. His football skills are great and he could also have flourished as a footballer. His uncle, Miguel Angel, was a great professional footballer for both the Spanish national team and Barcelona. Therefore, he had the mentorship and ability to move in that direction.

According to Nadal, choosing between football and tennis was one of the toughest decisions he ever made. His father also stated that he could have been a great footballer. However, in a footballing era dominated by Lionel Messi and Cristiano Ronaldo, he could have been overshadowed by them as they have done to other great footballers, such as Robert Lewandowski and Zlatan Ibrahimovic. The story of Nadal teaches us that focusing on one particular thing is critical to achieving greatness. He could not have achieved success if he kept dovetailing between football and tennis. Tennis is his 20% which accounted for over 80% of his success as an individual.

Applying The Pareto Principle To Goal Setting

Goal setting as an art depends on your skillfulness to make it effective. A fusion of the Pareto principle with goal setting will increase your chances of reaching your targets. It is essential that you are deliberate in your goals and how you intend to achieve them. Goal setting gives you the focus you need to detect distractions and avoid procrastination, and leveraging the Pareto Principle makes it a lethal combo.

Discover Your 20%

When you apply the Pareto Principle to goal setting, you will start by highlighting the things that matter to you. Your love for the game of soccer does not also have to become a career. It can just be something you do whenever you are less busy and want to have fun. It is likely Nadal still plays football once in a while. Yet, it is not likely that improving his football skills is one of his goals at the beginning of every year. Tennis is his 20% and he will most likely set targets in that regard.

It will be absurd for Nadal to have a target to score twenty goals in football every year when he is a professional tennis player. He will be more focused on fine-tuning his tennis techniques to score more points, defeat more competitors, and improve his ranking. Take a cue from this and discover your 20%. Your job and relationship with your loved ones should form a crucial part of this. It is a sign that your priorities are right when you set targets that can improve your productivity in your career.

Your interpersonal relationships might not be financially rewarding but you need their support for your mental health. Therefore, how you can improve your interpersonal relationships should be one of your goals. This can involve various activities that involve spending quality time with your friends and family. What matters is that you invest the most in your 20% which influences 80% of your success.

Chapter Five: Leveraging The Pareto Principle In Your Interpersonal Relationships

Buddhists believe the concept of self is a mirage because an individual is interconnected with several people. This is not far from the truth. An individual is an expression of the history of the universe, its evolution, and the contributions of family and friends of that person. The quality of our lives depends on the quality of our interpersonal relationships. Therefore, you cannot afford to take this aspect of your life for granted. This chapter will discuss how you can maintain and strengthen your interpersonal relationships by leveraging the Pareto Principle.

The Loss of Empathy In The Modern World

Loneliness is fast becoming one of the biggest problems of the modern world. According to a global survey on *Statista*, 33% of adults experience loneliness all over the world. Note that loneliness is not the same as being alone. We all want to be alone sometimes. You need it. It is recommended that you have times in your life when you are alone to reflect on the current situation in your life. You need to spend time alone to plan and think about the way forward in every aspect of your life. Nonetheless, it can be a sign of depression when you usually do not want to have people around you.

It is not shocking that many people feel lonely because we are fast becoming machines. We are always seeking a new celebrity only to reject them when they make mistakes or do things that do not augur well with us. We all make mistakes and celebrities are no different. They are human beings like us but we forget about that simply because they are famous. When rapper Kanye West opened up about his mental health, it became something many people found amusing.

In the same way, when Will Smith watched a TV show and heard his wife confess her infidelity and describe it as an entanglement, it became something many people used to make fun of him. Life is tough enough but it is getting worse because many people have lost empathy in the modern world. They find it exciting and amusing when famous people are struggling with certain aspects of their lives. It is their opportunity to convince themselves that money and fame cannot buy happiness. It is increasingly important that we have a community of loved ones that can support us emotionally in this cold, hard world.

Existing In A Community

During his observation of Aspen trees, Authur Brooks discovered that they are interconnected, which makes them more durable and resistant. He used this fact to explain the importance of building strong relationships with the people around us to increase our chances of living happily and meaningfully. It is preposterous and naive to think that we do not need anyone. Our decisions are indeed the most critical aspects of our experience in life. Yet, the actions and gestures of others also play crucial roles in determining our success in life.

Lionel Messi might be one of the greatest football players ever known. Yet, he had coaches and teammates that contributed massively to his success. Without them, he could not have achieved so much. At some point in Barcelona, his coach back then, Pep Guardiola, gave him the role of a false nine and sold older players like Ronaldinho and Samuel Eto'o which could have reduced his game time. These decisions created the platform for Messi to shine. The hard work and cooperation of his Barcelona and Argentina teammates were also crucial to his success in both his club and the national team.

He would be an ingrate if he did not acknowledge the efforts of those people who gave him the platform to use his skills effectively. We all need others and it is arrogant to argue otherwise. We are made to exist in a community of people who love and understand us. Life becomes more stressful and unrewarding when we find ourselves amid people who are insensitive and disrespect us. On the other hand, it is easy to be motivated and find reasons to be happy when you have loving and supportive people around you.

The Pareto Principle In Your Relationships

The crux of leveraging the Pareto Principle in your interpersonal relationships is discovering the 20% of people in your life that offer more value and investing more time and effort into those relationships. We are usually quick to refer to people we met recently as friends but this can be a grave mistake. This is the reason some people expose themselves to people who betray them and misplace their trust. Friendship has to be tested and proven. You might never know your true friends until the times you are in trouble.

If you cannot imagine how your current friends will treat you if you lose your job or lose access to some of the privileges you have, you have been spending your time with the wrong set of people. You should strive to be independent so that you will never be a burden to anyone. However, it is one of the greatest gifts to have people that can support you during periods when things are not going your way. You will find it easier to recover from sickness or any other challenges when you have people that are willing to give you the necessary support. When you find such people, never allow anything to ruin the relationship.

Cultivating Your Network Of Valuable People

It is not pleasant to have people around you that cannot offer you emotional and financial support during your dark days. However, you have a part to play in having such people in your life. The truth is that you will have fewer friends as you grow older because you will continue to discover your true friends over time. Yet, the way you treat the people around you also matters. You cannot be the type who gives excuses whenever your friends need you and expect them to take you seriously when you need their help.

You should be the kind of friend you want to have. If you want your friends to be loyal and committed to you, you should sow the seeds. Be that indispensable friend that everyone wants to have. Do not just seek the 20% of people among your friends and family that add the most value to your life. You should also be among the 20% in the lives of others that offer them the most significant value. People should not just tolerate you; they should want to be around you because you are a valuable human being. You can build yourself into that kind of person deliberately.

Chapter Six: Leveraging The Pareto Principle In Your Marriage

The institution of marriage is quickly losing its place in the modern world. The unacceptable rate of divorce tells the sad story of the state of marriage in our world today. Yet, marriage remains one of the most satisfying and helpful relationships when it works. There is nothing more beautiful than two people loving and supporting themselves while raising wonderful and independent children. I believe in marriage and this chapter will be dedicated to explaining how you can make it work by taking advantage of the Pareto Principle.

What Is Wrong With Our Marriages?

Marriage is increasingly becoming transactional in the modern world. It is as though people go in cautiously with one leg and leave the other leg outside. So, they quickly opt-out at any sign of trouble. Researchers predict that almost 50% of marriages in the US will end in divorce. Also, 41% of first marriages in the US end in divorce. It gets worse with second marriages. Over 60% of second marriages end in divorce. This is alarming and sad. Why is a relationship that was meant to end happily-ever-after, breaking up so easily?

This should bother us because of the impact it has on the children whose parents are divorced and society at large. Single parenting is difficult and it is usually not as effective as when both parents raise their kids together. Bringing the child of another person into a new home is not the easiest of situations for the child or the spouse. The fact that the child is not living with both parents is a cloud that will continue to linger and can affect the emotional and social development of the child.

Children from broken homes usually struggle with a sense of identity and might lack empathy because they were not raised in an atmosphere of love and kindness. They have seen their parents fight and suffer abuse, especially their mothers and this affects their worldview. Many of them become criminals and contribute to the many vices we have in our society today. Therefore, we cannot say it is none of our business if homes are crashing at an alarming rate. Directly or indirectly, we all suffer from the consequences of this unfortunate pattern in life today.

Learning From The Right Models

In these days of social media influencers, falsehoods and scripted lifestyles are the order of the day. Many people advertise products they do not ever use, all for the sake of monetary gain. Sadly, many younger people are learning about romantic relationships from the wrong set of people today and this is one of the problems we have with our society. Romantic relationships are notoriously made public today, especially when the partners are celebrities. Who does not love the romance of two celebrities displaying how much they love "each other" and themselves? However, these stunts do not usually end well.

It is full of pretense and show. After the charade of entertaining their fans, many of them will announce that they have broken up. Sometimes, the love affair has led to pregnancy and the birth of children. We are living in a dangerous era where having "baby mamas" is the norm and we have become very comfortable with this reality. Indeed, marriage involves a lot of commitment but it is worth it when you are fortunate enough to be with the right person. However, the desire to marry a celebrity has clouded the judgment of many people.

Their bid to prove to others that they married someone wealthy and famous has made them throw away every other crucial virtue, such as patience, empathy, endurance, resilience, and perseverance. We cannot continue this way because it is not working and is ruining our society. It is high time we started celebrating couples being together for over twenty, thirty, or even forty years. It is possible when we get our priorities right. Marriage should not be transactional. It should be a deliberate attempt by two people to create a future together that will allow them to raise wonderful children while living their dream.

The Pareto Effect On Your Marriage

We can build strong and enjoyable marriages by leveraging the Pareto Principle. Many marriages break down due to what the couples usually describe as "irreconcilable differences." People indeed change but there is no such thing as an irreconcilable difference if the two parties involved want the marriage to work. Someone once asked me what I think is the most important factor that can make a marriage work. I responded by saying that the couple decides to refuse to give up on their marriage (as well as mutual respect, which is often lacking?)

As long as the two parties are willing to keep the marriage going, with mutual respect, nothing can bring it to an end. However, in our generation, many people are no longer willing to persevere and exercise patience to make something work. Once there is a challenge, we are already seeking a change. This attitude is seen in our political approach, the way we support a football club, and also our relationships. If you are not yet married, the fact that you have many ex-partners is a red flag. If you also struggle to keep friends, it is an ominous sign that you might struggle to keep a marriage alive.

The mindset of irreconcilable differences begins from the way you treat your issues with your friends. You can know your tolerance, patience, and loyalty level from the way you treat your friends. No miracle will transform you into a new person after walking down the aisle. You should be deliberate about working on yourself. It is a costly assumption to think that you will treat your spouse better than your friends. The butterflies in your belly will eventually die a natural death overtime. It is the quality of friendship you have with your spouse that will be left.

Finding The 20% In Your Marriage

The key to keeping a positive atmosphere in your marriage is understanding your partner. All men are not the same and this also applies to women. It is a costly mistake to compare your spouse with another person. It hurts when someone compares you with others. So, why should you do the same to your spouse? It is recommended that you understand the love language of your spouse. It is not every person that values expensive gifts. Your spouse might prefer that you cook at home while doing it together and having fun.

Taking her out to a restaurant will not have the same value for such people. Therefore, you mustn't force your spouse to become what he or she is not, for you.

You should understand the 20% of things that matter the most to that person, which will determine 80% of his or her satisfaction. Discover them and do them more, rather than always trying to do things that satisfy you. Compromise is critical in any relationship. You should let the other person have his or her way, sometimes, as long as it does not contradict your core values.

Chapter Seven: Leveraging The Pareto Principle In Leadership

Based on career satisfaction statistics, the most productive employees are the ones that come to work every day with the intent to solve problems, achieve specific targets, and weather the storms associated with their jobs. Every leader wants such people in their team but it is easier said than done. This chapter will explore how you can leverage the Pareto Principle to achieve the best results as a leader in any capacity.

Leadership Is Key

> *"Everything rises and falls on leadership."*
>
> John C. Maxwell

The leadership of an organization or institution plays a significant role in determining its success. Leadership sets the goals, vision, and strategy of the team. A leader sets the target and develops a practical plan to achieve it. In the animated movie, *Angry Bird 2*, Red was desperate to lead a team of birds and pigs against the eagles. He was passionate and dedicated to the cause but it was obvious to the team members that he had no plan or clue regarding how to achieve the target. Note that leadership goes beyond leading an organization. As a parent, you are a leader to your children, and the husband is meant to offer leadership to his wife and children.

Regardless of the capacity, you can leverage the Pareto Principle to act as an exemplary leader. The key to using the Pareto Principle as a leader is discovering your key team members and the most productive activities of your team. Once you discover the key members of your team that are willing to achieve the mission and vision of the team, they should be your main focus. It is a waste of time to spend time and effort on people that are not willing to grow and move in the same direction you are heading as a team. It is best to sideline such people temporarily or permanently.

Leading With The Pareto Principle

Unless you are a dictator, people are supposed to follow you because they trust you and believe in you. They will lose faith in your leadership if you do not display the capacity to get results. The Pareto Principle can help you in this regard. You can take advantage of the Pareto Principle as a leader in the following ways:

Identify The Most Effective Team Members

People are not all motivated in the same way in the workplace. Some people are only motivated by the financial gain involved in a task, while some see the workplace as an opportunity to solve problems and offer value. Of course, such people have to be paid but they are usually willing to go the extra mile to ensure that the targets of the team are met. Every leader wants to have such people but the reality is that such people are rare. However, it is not impossible to find them.

It is a great leadership skill to know how to focus more on the most effective members of your team without disliking and rejecting the less effective ones. You will end up creating an atmosphere of discord when you make it obvious that you have favourites among your team members. This is also crucial in parenting. Your kids should not know that you have a favourite child. It can lead to an unhealthy comparison among your children that can destroy the bond of the family. You will regret it if you are the reason your children hate themselves.

Avoid Sentiments

You will send the wrong message to the people that are productive and loyal to you as a leader when you reward people that are not showing a similar level of commitment and loyalty. My mentor once told me that you will discourage your loyal followers when you reward the people that are disloyal to you. This sentiment is usually due to the capability of such people. We all want to have people that have the expertise to carry out certain tasks effectively. Yet, you should not sacrifice capability for loyalty because it is easier to find talented people than to find loyal people.

Loyal and committed people will eventually become experts if you invest in them. Make it your duty to train them and help them improve their skills. When you are responsible for training them, they feel they owe you and this increases their loyalty and commitment to you. Everyone does not have to start their own business. It is productive and satisfying when you work with people that will not treat you like a machine and allow you to maximize your potential. Try to be that leader that gives people around him or her the confidence to solve problems and grow as individuals.

Keep The Door Open

It is frustrating when you lead people that are not cooperating or responding as expected. You should have the means of punishing ineptitude and rebellion and you have to be consistent in this regard. Once you punish a team member for an action, any other team member found wanting must get the same treatment. You open the door for your team members to doubt you or even rebel against you when your actions are not consistent. In the same way, you should be consistent with your reward for good behaviour.

Punish offenders and defaulters but it is not recommended that you shut the door on anyone. In other words, if a defaulter is willing to make amends and do better, it is recommended that you allow such a person to retrace his or her steps. This is critical in parenting. The fact that a person was ineffective or ruined a task does not mean that the person will never be able to make amends. Giving people the opportunity to atone for their mistakes is one of the ways you can build a strong relationship with your followers and children. Reunions are usually beautiful. It makes the offender want to strive to ensure that what went wrong the last time does not repeat itself.

Set The Right Examples

Leadership should not be coercive. Rather, it should be exemplary. It is hypocritical to tell people to do the things you do not do. This approach will make you lose the respect of your followers. If you are fond of breaking the rules of the team because you are the leader, your followers will revolt against you. They will grumble when you instruct them and will not be motivated to carry out your directives.

You will end up threatening them or coercing them when you do not lead by example. Submission and obedience flow naturally from your followers when you are a good example of the values you expect them to uphold. Therefore, if you want to have people that will be committed to your vision as a leader, you must embody the vision. This can be demanding but it is one of the requirements of leading people.

Chapter Eight: Leveraging The Pareto Principle To Find Meaning And Happiness

Despite the number of unhappy people in the world today, happiness is not elusive. It is either we pursue it wrongly or do not want it. Still, at the end of our lives, we will end up realizing that none of our achievements are more important than the feeling of satisfaction that comes from living a happy and meaningful life. In this chapter, we will discuss how you can take advantage of the Pareto Principle in your pursuit of happiness and meaning.

Happiness or Success

In *From Strength To Strength,* author Brooks discussed his experience with a successful businesswoman. She explained how she had been struggling with happiness and fulfillment despite her success. She had reached a point in her professional career where it was declining but she did not want to quit the job. When Brooks highlighted what she needed to do to be happy, she said she preferred to feel important rather than happy. As strange as this might sound, this is the state of mind of many people in the world today.

Chase Success Sensibly And Responsibly

Motivational speakers only tell us to chase our dreams but they never warn us that success is addictive. They also never tell us that our success will decline and we will lose the recognition we used to enjoy at some point in our lives. No wonder many famous and successful people are depressed today. At the height of it, some of them commit suicide. Chef Antony Bourdain is a perfect example of this. He once proudly told the *New Yorker* in an interview that he had the best job in the world. He was a celebrity of note who took part in two TV shows, *Parts Unknown* and *No Reservations*.

Nonetheless, the unbelievable happened on June 8, 2018. This famous chef hung himself in a hotel room in France! It was discovered that he had issues with his relationship and was battling alcohol addiction. He was a workaholic and this could have contributed to the other issues. If a person works so hard that he does not have time for his loved ones, such a person will inevitably experience loneliness and have a gap in his life that success can never fill.

You do not have to choose between success and happiness because it is possible to have both. The problem is that many people are willing to sacrifice anything, including their health and family, to become celebrities. They are addicted to the limelight and are desperate for recognition. You should strive to be the best possible in your career but it does not have to be at the expense of your mental health and relationships.

The Pareto Principle Formula For Happiness

According to the Harvard Study of Adult Development, relationships are what contribute the most to our level of happiness. Therefore, it would be unwise of us if we do not place importance on this aspect of our lives. This shows that the relationship aspect is the 20% that affects 80% of our happiness. Indeed, life can be unfair and full of jeopardy. How do you explain the deafness of Ludwig van Beethoven at the point he was beginning to blossom into a world-class musician? To his credit, he did not allow the situation to weigh him down but found another way to showcase his talents.

Life is full of stressful and sad events, such as the death of a loved one, job loss, sickness, and divorce. Yet, with a strong network of people who cares about you, you can weather any storm. Authur Brooks describes being deliberate about investing in your interpersonal relationships as "cultivating your Aspen grove." This is crucial to your happiness. Evidence from research and anecdotal data has proven this. Yet, many people prefer to spend more time with fanciful things that do not offer lasting satisfaction, such as digital devices and social media, (that only cater to their escapism needs?).

Initially, I thought playing games alone was a great way to relax. However, I found out that it contributes negatively to my feeling of relaxation when I spend quality time with it. Surfing the Internet by visiting social media pages can also have an impact on you. Some people develop what is known as the Fear Of Missing Out (FOMO) due to their social media addiction. FOMO is a feeling of anxiety an individual displays because he or she feels that they are missing out on some novel experiences whenever they are not on social media.

Do What Makes You Happy

Normally, you have several activities lined up for a typical day. You might want to cook, meditate, work, pray, visit a friend, do your dishes, do your laundry, and prepare for a presentation. Most of the things we do in a typical day are done because they are important. We do them to keep up with life. However, they do not necessarily play significant roles in our happiness. For example, I cook because it is healthy and also a means to save money. Yet, I do not like to cook.

I feel it is stressful and requires time that could have been spent on other things. I am sure that there are people that have a different opinion about this. I have friends who feel happy whenever they cook, especially when cooking for others. They enjoy the compliments they get from people who enjoy their meals but that does not appeal to me. You need to understand your uniqueness and discover the 20% of things that contribute to 80% of your happiness. For me, having intellectual and faith-based conversations with intelligent people, makes me feel alive.

I thoroughly enjoy doing it. I can go hungry a whole day without thinking about it when I am involved in a meaningful and intellectual conversation with a person on the same page. Playing sports comes close also. It is recommended that you discover yours and spend more time doing them. Life is too short to be lived under intense pressure. Do the things that are needful because it is a sign that you are a responsible person. Yet, you should not cheat yourself out of relaxation and pleasure. Have your me-time once in a while and enjoy the moment. You owe that to yourself for being amazing.

Conclusion

This journey began by stating the fact that you can leverage the Pareto Principle, which is based on recognizing the most productive areas and investing in them, in every aspect of your life. We proceeded by discussing how you can leverage this principle in your career by discovering your passion and investing in it to give you a higher chance of job satisfaction and success in your professional endeavours subsequent chapters, we explored how you can leverage this principle in stress management, goal setting, interpersonal relationships, marriage, leadership, and in the pursuit of a happy and meaningful life. The emphasis of each chapter is based on the foundation that you need to discover the 20% most productive aspect in your life that can offer you the most value.

The simplicity of these tips might tempt you to downplay their effectiveness but that is not the best approach. It is recommended that you practice what you learned, to achieve more while doing less in every area of your life. You deserve to enjoy all that life offers in every respect. So, why settle for less? The Pareto Principle can be your winning formula. Never forget that today is a great day to be alive!

References

Boyd, D. (2021, February 9). *Workplace Stress.* The American Institute of Stress. Retrieved March 12, 2022, from https://www.stress.org/workplace-stress

Carla, T. (2022, March 12). *How to Apply the 80–20 Rule.* Investopedia. Retrieved March 12, 2022, from https://www.investopedia.com/terms/1/80-20-rule.asp

Finra. (2021, April 28). *Large Number of Americans Reported Financial Anxiety and Stress Even Before the Pandemic | FINRA.org.* Retrieved March 12, 2022, from https://www.finra.org/media-center/newsreleases/2021/large-number-americans-reported-financial-anxiety-and-stress-even

Mayo Clinic (2021, March 24). *Stress symptoms: Effects on your body and behaviour.* (2021, March 24). Mayo Clinic. Retrieved March 12, 2022, from https://www.mayoclinic.org/healthy-lifestyle/stress-management/in-depth/stress-symptoms/art-20050987?reDate=12032022

Michael, M. (2011). *PolitiFact - Michael Moore says 400 Americans have more wealth than half of all Americans combined.* @politifact. Retrieved March 12, 2022, from https://www.politifact.com/factchecks/2011/mar/10/michael-moore/michael-moore-says-400-americans-have-more-wealth-/

Mineo, L. (2018, November 26). *Over nearly 80 years, Harvard study has been showing how to live a healthy and happy life.* Harvard Gazette. Retrieved March 12, 2022, from https://news.harvard.edu/gazette/story/2017/04/over-nearly-80-years-harvard-study-has-been-showing-how-to-live-a-healthy-and-happy-life/

Pew Research. (2021, September 28). *3. How Americans view their jobs.* Pew Research Center's Social & Demographic Trends Project. Retrieved March 12, 2022, from https://www.pewresearch.org/social-trends/2016/10/06/3-how-americans-view-their-jobs/

Robison, B. V. G. A. J. (2022, February 18). *The "Great Resignation" Is Really the "Great Discontent."* Gallup.Com. Retrieved

March 12, 2022, from https://www.gallup.com/workplace/351545/great-resignation-really-great-discontent.aspx

Statista. (2021, November 4). *Feeling of loneliness among adults 2021, by country*Retrieved March 12, 2022, from https://www.statista.com/statistics/1222815/loneliness-among-adults-by-country/

Valizadeh, L., Farnam, A., & Rahkar Farshi, M. (2012). Investigation of Stress

Symptoms among Primary School Children. *Journal of caring sciences*, *1*(1),

25–30. https://doi.org/10.5681/jcs.2012.004

Wilkinson & Finkbeiner, LLP. (2022, March 3). *Divorce Statistics and Facts | What Affects Divorce Rates in the U.S.?* Retrieved March 12, 2022, from https://www.wf-lawyers.com/divorce-statistics-and-facts/

Thank you for reading this book!

If you found this book helpful, I would be grateful if you would **post an honest review on Amazon** so this book can reach other supportive readers like you!

All you need to do is digitally flip to the back and leave your review. Or visit amazon.com/author/senseipauldavid click the correct book cover and click on the blue link next to the yellow stars that say, "customer reviews."

As always...
It's a great day to be alive!

Get/Share Our FREE All-Ages Mental Health Book Now!

FREE Self-Development Book for Every Family

senseiselfdevelopment.senseipublishing.com

Click Below or Search Amazon for Another Book In This Series Or Visit:

www.amazon.com/author/senseipauldavid

www.senseipublishing.com

@senseipublishing
#senseipublishing

Check out our **recommendations** for other books for adults & kids plus other great resources by visiting www.senseipublishing.com/resources/

Join Our Publishing Journey!

If you would like to receive FREE BOOKS, special offers, please visit www.senseipublishing.com and join our newsletter by entering your email address in the pop-up box

Follow Our Engaging Blog NOW! senseipauldavid.ca

Get Our FREE Books Today!

Click & Share the Link Below

FREE Self-Development Book
senseiselfdevelopment.senseipublishing.com

FREE BONUS!!!
Experience Over 25 FREE Engaging Guided Meditations!

Prized Skills & Practices for Adults & Kids. Help Restore Deep-Sleep, Lower Stress, Improve Posture, Navigate Uncertainty & More.

Download the Free Insight Timer App and click the link below:
http://insig.ht/sensei_paul

About Sensei Publishing

Sensei Publishing commits itself to helping people of all ages transform into better versions of themselves by providing high-quality and research-based self-development books with an emphasis on mental health and guided meditations. Sensei Publishing offers well-written e-books, audiobooks, paperbacks and online courses that simplify complicated but practical topics in line with its mission to inspire people towards positive transformation.

It's a great day to be alive!

About the Author

I create simple & transformative eBooks & Guided Meditations for Adults & Children proven to help navigate uncertainty, solve niche problems & bring families closer together.

I'm a former finance project manager, private pilot, jiu-jitsu instructor, musician & former University of Toronto Fitness Trainer. I prefer a science-based approach to focus on these & other areas in my life to stay humble & hungry to evolve. I hope you enjoy my work and I'd love to hear your feedback.

- It's a great day to be alive!
Sensei Paul David

Scan & Follow/Like/Subscribe: Facebook, Instagram, YouTube: @senseipublishing

Scan using your phone/iPad camera for Social Media Visit us at www.senseipublishing.com and sign up for our newsletter to learn more about our exciting books and to experience our FREE Guided Meditations for Kids & Adults.

www.ingramcontent.com/pod-product-compliance
Lightning Source LLC
Chambersburg PA
CBHW071115030426
42336CB00013BA/2101